The Women's Movement and Young Women Today

The Women's Movement and Young Women Today

A Hot Issue

Barbara J. Berg

Enslow Publishers, Inc.

40 Industrial Road   PO Box 38
Box 398   Aldershot
Berkeley Heights, NJ 07922 Hants GU12 6BP
USA   UK

http://www.enslow.com

Library of Congress Cataloging-in-Publication Data

Berg, Barbara J.
The women's movement and young women today : a hot issue /
Barbara J. Berg.
p. cm. — (Hot issues)
Includes bibliographical references and index.
Summary: Explores the history of the women's movement
through the twentieth century and discusses the many issues
facing women today.
ISBN 0-7660-1200-X
1. Feminism—United States—Juvenile literature.
2. Feminism—United States—History—20th century—Juvenile
literature. 3. Women—United States—Juvenile literature.
4. Teenage girls—United States—Juvenile literature. [1. Feminism.]
I. Title. II. Series.
HQ1426 .B4287 2000
305.42'0973—dc21   98-50274
                                                       CIP
                                                       AC

Printed in the United States of America

10 9 8 7 6 5 4 3 2 1

To Our Readers:
All Internet addresses in this book were active and appropriate when we
went to press. Any comments or suggestions can be sent by e-mail to
Comments@enslow.com or to the address on the back cover.

Illustration Credits: AP/Wide World Photos, pp. 21, 24, 31, 35, 43,
49, 56; © Corel Corporation, pp. 3, 6; National Archives, p. 16

Cover Illustration: National Organization of Women

Contents

Smart, cute, courageous, dumb, strong, tall, blonde, tough, honest, manipulate, timid, emotional, hysterical, rational, pretty

Lizzie Cobb gave these words to her seventh grade English class and asked the girls and boys to use them in a series of sentences. Some of their responses included the following:

"The blonde girl who gave the dumb answer in class tried to act cute when the teacher corrected her."

"Eric is a tall blonde basketball player who is honest in class and tough on the courts."

"The tall blonde girl was pretty enough to manipulate all the boys she knew."

"Joanie decided to be really courageous and ask her coach if she could play, but when she saw how good the other team looked, she became timid and sat out the game on the bench."

Sentence after sentence portrayed the girls as emotional, hysterical, and timid, and the boys as rational, smart, and strong. Surprised by her students' responses, Cobb asked her class if they could think of women who were courageous, strong, smart, and honest. Immediately hands went up. "Sally Ride" (first woman in space), "Dominique Dawes" (first African-American woman to win the United States Gymnastic Championship), "Janet Reno" (United States attorney general), and "Toni Morrison" (winner of a Nobel prize in literature), the students responded.

Cobb's students named quite a few women who possessed what they considered traditional male qualities such as courage, strength, and determination. However, the students thought of these as exceptional individuals who did not really represent the rest of their sex.

Why was this so? Why did Cobb's students still think that there were basic personality traits that were female and others that were male? And why did they cast women in negative and inferior roles?

Cobb's class came up with some answers to these questions just by examining practices in their own school.

➢ No female student had ever been elected president of the student body, and girls were not in positions of leadership in extracurricular activities.

➢ Girls were underrepresented in honor math and science classes.

➢ Many teachers called on boys more than on girls in their classes.

➢ Many girls, as young as nine years old, were vigorously dieting, some developing serious eating disorders that made them appear small and fragile.

No wonder these seventh graders continued to think that there were some qualities that belong only to girls and other qualities or character traits that are associated only with boys. These stereotypes—seeing boys as having certain qualities and girls as having others—made it hard for Cobb's students to think of girls as strong and successful. Unfortunately, the patterns they observed are not confined to their school, but exist nationwide as the following facts indicate:

➤ Reflections of Risk, a survey of thirty-six thousand girls and boys published by the Minnesota Women's Fund, found adolescent girls to be under more stress than boys.[1]

➤ Girls are significantly more prone to depression than boys. The higher rates begin at age twelve and persist through adolescence.[2]

➤ There has been an alarming increase, over the last five years, in the number of teenage girls who have started smoking, have become sexually active, and have contracted sexually transmitted diseases.[3]

➤ One teenage girl in ten gets pregnant every year, and nearly 75 percent of those who become mothers at age seventeen or younger do not finish high school.[4]

➤ Between 30 and 40 percent of adolescent girls from all backgrounds have endured some physical abuse during the course of dating; 81 percent report being subjected to unwanted sexual behavior in school.[5]

➤ Boys continue to outscore girls in both math and verbal sections of the SATs, and they account for two out of three Merit Scholarship finalists; boys also register higher scores on eleven out of fourteen national achievement tests, and these differences become greater on the Graduate Record Exams.[6]

> Girls are lagging behind boys in computer sciences; fewer girls than boys enroll in computer classes, and those who do often drop out before the end of the term.[7]

These statistics present an image of women's status or position in America that is disheartening to anyone who believes in fairness. Historically, women have had fewer rights and a lower status than men have had. But for over one hundred fifty years, groups of women seeking to improve the lives of women have struggled to end discrimination against members of their sex and to expand women's rights.

There have been two main waves of women's movements in America. The first wave, which began in the 1840s, concentrated on winning voting rights for women. The second wave developed during the 1960s. Its goals were to expand women's legal rights and to change attitudes about women's roles in the family and in the workplace. These two waves of the women's movement had different goals and methods, but each one gained greater freedom for women.

There is, however, a long way to go before women enjoy full equality with men. As Cobb's students realized, women continue to be second-class citizens. Women are still discriminated against in many ways and in many places in American society. For example, a recent front-page article in *The New York Times* described large-scale discrimination against women professors at the Massachusetts Institute of Technology (M.I.T.), the most famous and respected university for science and technology in the country.[8] Compared with their male colleagues, women professors received lower salaries, fewer promotions, and infrequent invitations to participate on important committees.[9] Although there are more women college professors nationwide than on the past twenty years, there is still a bias against them.[10]

What explains this discrimination? Why did it not disappear after one hundred fifty years of women fighting for their rights? How can girls and women work to make life better for themselves and for other women?

The answers to these questions lie in an understanding of the history of the women's movement in America. When women know their history, it enables them to see that discrimination against them comes from many sources: unexamined traditions and customs, faulty "scientific" theories, economic difficulties, and the interest some men have in keeping power to themselves.

During the past one hundred fifty years, thousands of women from different backgrounds have struggled to bring about many of the rights and freedoms women enjoy today. The history of women in this country is rich with role models in courage, strength, determination, creativity, and achievement. Their stories prove beyond a doubt that there are no female traits and no male traits: only human traits.

Chapter 1

Background of Today's Women's Movement

In 1797, Isabella Graham, a middle-class woman living in New York City started an organization to help less fortunate members of her own sex. The organization was made up of only women. This was the first benevolent or charitable organization managed by women in the United States. Its members named it the Society for the Relief of Poor Widows with Small Children. Although the members of the society had very simple goals—to distribute food and firewood to the poor—they were criticized by men, and even some other women, for engaging in behavior that was not considered proper for members of their sex.

Throughout the eighteenth and nineteenth centuries, women were confined to the traditional roles of wife and mother. They were supposed to be concerned only with their own households. Society was divided into a private sphere, in which women were to spend their lives, and the public sphere of higher education, politics, and professions that was reserved for men. Women were not allowed to sign contracts or to own property. Those women who crossed over into the public sphere risked their reputations and often the goodwill of their family and friends. But Isabella Graham refused to give up her charitable work. She convinced other women to be as determined as she was. After many years, she finally won acceptance for her work among the poor.

During the first half of the nineteenth century, as rapid urbanization (development and growth of cities) and industrialization (changing from small craft production to large-scale production often done in factories) brought huge numbers of poor and homeless women into our nation's cities, other women followed Isabella Graham's example. Hundreds of female charitable organizations flourished in New York City, Boston, Philadelphia, and as far west as Ohio. The members often worked with governmental officials and began to ask for better wages, education, and fairer property laws for women. As women began to gain confidence in their abilities, they began to demand more rights.

With the founding of the Troy Female Seminary (now the Emma Willard School) in 1821, girls could have a high school education.[1] Oberlin Collegiate Institute (now Oberlin College) opened in 1833 as the first coeducational college in America.[2] Some states allowed married women to sign contracts and own property. Slowly, women widened the boundaries of their sphere.

Many members of female urban charitable organizations also participated in the growing number of antislavery or abolition societies during the 1830s and 1840s. Two of these women were Lucretia Mott and Elizabeth Cady Stanton. They met each other in London after they, along with the other female delegates, were barred from attending the World Anti-Slavery Convention in 1840. Mott and Stanton were shocked and angry that male abolitionists, who wanted to free the slaves, refused to grant women the right to be present and speak at a convention. Mott and Stanton decided to dedicate themselves to gaining greater rights for women.

The first women's rights convention in America, held at Seneca Falls in 1848, came about through the efforts of Mott and Stanton. The Declaration of Rights and Sentiments, adopted by the convention, called for women to receive "all the rights and privileges which belong to them as citizens of the United States." The convention specifically called for women to be granted the right to vote.[3] Although women continued to hold meetings and conventions, the Civil War (1860–1865) interrupted their efforts.

The Right to Vote

The demand for women's suffrage (the right to vote) resurfaced after the end of the Civil War. Two main organizations, the National Woman Suffrage Association (NWSA) and the American Woman Suffrage Association (AWSA), championed the cause by holding conventions and distributing literature.[4] In 1890, these two associations merged to form the National American Women Suffrage Association. They began to use some of the methods of the British suffragists (those who support women's suffrage), such as outdoor speeches and parades. These new methods proved very effective.[5] In 1920, responding to a variety of pressures, the

United States adopted the Nineteenth Amendment to the Constitution, giving women the right to vote.[6]

With winning the vote, the first wave of the women's movement in America ebbed. Many people assumed that there was no longer a need for a women's movement. It took World War II (1939–1945) and its aftermath to convince them that they were wrong.

World War II

World War II brought great changes for American women. With the men away fighting, women were given the opportunity to play a variety of new roles. They entered the labor force in unprecedented numbers, joined the military, and assumed positions of leadership in their communities.

Matty Shaw, who was twenty-four years old in 1943, recalled her life in New York City during the war:

> I never felt tired even though I was holding a paying job for the first time in my life. I got a job in an office, but many of my girlfriends were working in factories, most in war industries. At the end of the day a whole bunch of us went out together. All the restaurants were jammed and there was an excitement in the air. People were all talking about the war and we felt a part of what was happening.[7]

Matty Shaw was one of some 6 million women who entered the labor force during the war. American women have worked throughout our nation's history as teachers, nurses, and secretaries. But the women war-workers were different. During World War II the United States government, joined by the news media, launched a campaign to convince women that they could do jobs that were traditionally thought of as only for men.[8]

"Rosie the Riveter," a young woman dressed in overalls, her hair tied up under a bandanna, became a national symbol of patriotism. Her picture graced magazine covers and posters emphasizing women's civic duty to work at jobs that commonly were done by men. Rosie was not only a riveter, she also welded, cut laths (large sheets of building material), loaded shells, and used acetylene torches (torches that get their heat from burning a hot bright gas). "Girls who started working during World War II," said economist Caroline Bird, "never learned that some jobs 'belong' to men and others to women."[9]

Women from different backgrounds, many of whom would not have been hired before the war, benefited from the manpower shortage. African-American women and American Indian women, older women, and married women were now welcomed into the workforce. African-American women, for example, who had worked mainly as maids or farmhands now were able to find jobs in other areas. Poet Maya Angelou became the first African-American streetcar conductor in San Francisco during the war. The salaries of wartime workers, while not equal to those given to men for the same work, were still higher than what women received before the war.

Women also helped the war effort through branches of the armed forces: army—Women's Army Corps (WACS), nursing corps; navy—Women Accepted for Volunteer Emergency Service (WAVES), nursing corps; Coast Guard—SPARS (from the motto *Semper paratus*, always ready); and

*R*osie the Riveter was introduced as a symbol of patriotic womanhood in the 1940s. Her image inspired women to join the workforce during World War II.

Marines—Marine Corps Women's Reserve (MCWR). Approximately three hundred fifty thousand women served in these different branches, and another thousand flew commercial air force transport planes for the Women's Airforce Service Pilots (WASPS).[10]

Expanded Roles

Women's new roles gave them a greater sense of importance within their own communities. American-Indian women, for example, became key participants in the National Congress of American Indians established in 1944 to promote better communication among the tribes.[11]

While the war provided women with a new earning power and feelings of accomplishment, working conditions were often unfavorable to them. Many women were subjected to unwanted sexual attention at work, creating a hostile environment. Working mothers faced particular hardships because the government did little to provide day care, and women frequently had difficulty making their own arrangements for their children while they worked.

In spite of the challenges, most women wanted to remain at their jobs even when the war was over.[12] When the war ended in 1945, however, women were asked to leave their jobs to make room for the returning servicemen. The nation struggled to leave the war emergency behind and concentrate on peace. But almost at once, America and the Soviet Union became locked in tense and increasingly hostile interactions known as the Cold War, which lasted from 1945 to about 1991.

The Flight to the Suburbs

As the Cold War continued, the possibility of a Soviet nuclear attack haunted the United States. Many Americans, yearning for security, found it within their families. Home became a haven, a place where Americans could feel safe. Helped by government aid for home building, mortgages, and support for highway construction, along with stable salaries in the booming postwar economy, many white middle-class men were able to become suburban homeowners.

By 1946, the majority of the nation's families lived in homes they owned. This powerful commitment to family life had important implications for women. Women started marrying at a younger age than their mothers. The birthrate soared to a twentieth-century high after more than a hundred years of steady decline. This produced the famous Baby Boom that lasted for twenty years. Women did not look to college to provide them with necessary education and skills. Many women joked that the only degree they wanted was their "MRS" (which stands for Missus, the then common prefix to a married woman's last name). Once married, the lines of responsibility were clear. The husband was the sole wage earner, and the wife kept house and cared for the children.[13]

Rosie the Riveter was replaced by the suburban housewife. With no paying jobs, women were encouraged to make housekeeping their careers. They were financially dependent on their husbands. Husbands gave wives allowances for their spending needs, frequently keeping a close watch on how the money was spent.

In *I Love Lucy*, a popular television sitcom of the

era, many episodes revolved around Lucy's clever ploys to get money from her husband, Ricky. Real life was often not quite so funny. Women complained about feeling worthless and demeaned by having to ask and account for funds. To some women, suburban living was isolating and lonely. In her research on the 1950s, sociologist Helen Lopata found that at no other time in history was the individual mother and her children so cut off from other adults.[14] Brought up to believe in the American dream, suburban housewives wondered why they were so unhappy.

Over the next twenty years, American women from many different backgrounds would question their roles in society. The first group to protest their status were African-American women, whose struggle produced profound and lasting changes in American society.

The Civil Rights Movement

African-American women faced sexual and racial discrimination. Often married to men with poorly paying jobs, African-American women continued to seek whatever employment they could find. This search for a better life led many African Americans to leave the segregated rural south and travel north. In northern cities, masses of African-American men and women experienced life outside of the segregated system (separate facilities—schools, houses, restaurants—for blacks and whites) of the south. For the first time, large numbers of African Americans voted, giving hope to their southern friends and relatives that one day they too could exercise their rights as citizens. Hopes were further fed by the Supreme Court decision *Brown* v. *The Board of*

Education in 1954, declaring school segregation unconstitutional. Television also played a part, enabling many African Americans to see the remarkable display of white affluence on the screen. More aware than ever of their relative deprivation, African Americans across the nation were poised on the threshold of protest.

In December 1955, Rosa Parks triggered the boycott of the Montgomery, Alabama, bus system. She refused to give up her seat to a white passenger and was sent to jail. Her action helped start the civil rights movement in the United States.

While Parks was waiting for her trial, a group of women wrote and distributed flyers urging everyone to protest the arrest by refusing to ride the buses. A young minister, Martin Luther King, Jr., who had recently moved to Alabama, championed the boycott and urged nonviolent resistance. King's eloquent speeches quickly gained him recognition as the leader of the nonviolent wing of the civil rights movement. The Montgomery bus boycott, however, could not have continued without the commitment of hundreds of women. Refusing to yield to white pressure to break the boycott, these women, for a full year, walked many miles from their homes to their places of employment and, after a long, tiring workday, back again.

Success came when the Supreme Court ruled that racial segregation in public places such as buses, stores, and restaurants was unconstitutional. Still, most businesses in the South did not comply with this ruling and refused to admit African Americans to their establishments.

Voter registration became an important goal of the growing civil rights movement. Through a

*R*osa Parks sits in a 1950s-era bus in Montgomery, Alabama, on December 2, 1995, to commemorate the fortieth anniversary of her arrest for refusing to give up her seat.

combination of phony requirements, intimidation, and acts of violence, southern bigots effectively kept African Americans from voting for almost seventy-five years. Until Fannie Lou Hamer, a Mississippi sharecropper (a tenant farmer who works the land and receives a share of the value of the crops for his or her labor) who held three other jobs just to feed her children, attended a voter registration rally, she did not know that African Americans even had the right to vote. When the leader asked for volunteers to go to the state capital, she raised her hand. "The only thing they could do was kill me and it seemed like they'd been tryin' to do that a little bit at a time ever since I could remember."[15]

Because of her civil rights activities, Hamer lost her jobs and was shot at, jailed, and beaten. But she did not give up marching for justice until the Voting Rights Act was passed in 1965. The struggles and successes of the civil rights movement inspired women in different parts of the nation to fight for greater rights within society. While the civil rights movement brought about a new awareness of race in America, many of the movements that followed it would bring the issue of gender to public attention in a new and powerful way.

Chapter 2

Milestones of the Women's Movement

The second wave of the women's movement grew out of the civil rights movement and the protests against America's foreign policy in the 1950s–1970s. In November 1961, fifty thousand American housewives staged a massive protest against the Cold War. Calling their movement Women Strike for Peace, these women met with government officials and asked them to demand "An End to the Arms Race. Not the Human Race."[1]

In response to this growing activism of women, President John F. Kennedy appointed a Commission on the Status of Women, which was chaired by Eleanor Roosevelt. In 1963, the Commission's report described many areas of discrimination against women, particularly in employment and in the lack of social services such as child care. It highlighted policies such as separate help wanted listings for male and female jobs. Coincidentally, in the same year as the report, the book *The Feminine Mystique* was published. Betty Friedan wrote the book after interviewing suburban housewives forced out of public life and paid work after World War II and into the domestic sphere. Women told Friedan about their loneliness, their depression, and their sense of uselessness. Friedan launched a campaign for meaningful work outside of the home as a way to empower women.

All this set the stage for the inclusion of Title VII to the 1964 Civil Rights Act, which made discrimination on the basis of sex illegal, along with discrimination based on race, color, and religion. In order to investigate claims against employers, the Equal Employment Opportunities Commission (EEOC) was established. The EEOC, however, was so slow to look at women's claims of bias that Betty Friedan founded the National Organization for

*B*etty Friedan started the National Organization for Women to support women's efforts in the workplace. She is shown here in 1966 organizing a strike.

Women (NOW) to support women's efforts in the workplace. NOW, which emphasizes individual rights and equal participation in the workplace, appealed largely to middle-class women.

At the same time, younger women were questioning their place in American society. Many college women had traveled south in the summers of 1964 and 1965 to participate in the civil rights movement. Others, remaining in the north, had joined a new organization called Students for a Democratic Society (SDS). SDS sponsored community projects such as free day care centers for children of working mothers and food collectives where food could be purchased more cheaply than in grocery stores. Women students across the country were developing organizational and leadership skills, finding role models, and taking risks. Many of these women joined with men to challenge the war in Vietnam.

Along with men, women planned rallies, initiated fund-raising drives, and marched on Washington, D.C. However, they were hardly ever granted positions of leadership. Instead, they were expected to do the typing and make the coffee. Any attempt to better the position of women was dismissed by male coworkers.

Women Take Charge

These young women began to realize that women's liberation, or freedom from discriminatory laws and practices, could only come through their own efforts. Drawing on their organizing skills and their networks of activist women across the country, they set up small group discussions and began a process they called consciousness raising (CR). In these groups, women shared their experiences at school and work and in the home. Deborah, a member of a group in Washington, D.C., recalled:

> I confided how one of my professors was always telling me what nice legs I had whenever I went to speak to him about my work. I had never mentioned this to anyone, but three other members of my group immediately began to relate similar encounters.[2]

They began to understand that their individual experiences were part of a larger framework. Women began to explore the political meaning of their personal experiences. Sexism can be defined as any way in which women are kept as second-class citizens. By working together, women believed that they could and would change the world. "Sisterhood is Powerful" became the rallying cry for the movement fighting to end sexist institutions and practices and achieve full equality for women.

Changes in Society

Many books, articles, and speakers explored the meaning and impact of sexism in nearly every aspect of our society. Most professions, but especially law and medicine, came under sharp attack. Many women complained of not being taken seriously when they talked to male doctors about their physical problems. Some male doctors told women patients that they were "being hysterical." Other doctors treated grown women like little girls and did not give them enough information. A group of women, angry at this kind of treatment, became determined to find out all they could about women's health care. In 1971, they distributed their findings in a book. *Our Bodies/Ourselves* was a complete sourcebook about women's bodies and life stages. By providing women with much-needed knowledge about their bodies and how to care for them, the book encouraged women to take a more active role in their own heath care.[3]

Feminists, people who support the goals of women's liberation, also expanded the services available to women, including women's health clinics and rape crisis centers, and fought for more research into safe, effective birth control methods (the birth control pill on the market since 1960 had several serious side effects).

The most far-reaching court decision affecting women's lives was the Supreme Court case of *Roe v. Wade* in 1973. Jane Roe is the fictitious name for a young single pregnant woman denied an abortion in Texas in 1969. Texas law would allow abortions only if the woman's life was in danger. Roe sued in an attempt to prove that the law was unconstitutional. In this specific case, the Supreme Court ruled that a state may not prohibit abortion during the first three months of pregnancy and may do so during the second three months only under certain conditions.[4]

Feminists wanted women to enter medicine and other traditionally male fields. However, as late as 1970, college men outnumbered women 8 to 1 in expressing interest in careers in engineering, law, and medicine. By the mid-1970s, however, the number of women planning to enter traditionally feminine careers such as elementary school teaching and nursing fell from 31 percent to 10 percent. By the mid-1980s, students entering medical, law, and business schools were 40 percent female, and at some schools the numbers were up to about 50 percent.[5]

WORKING MOTHERS ON THE RISE

JUNE 1996

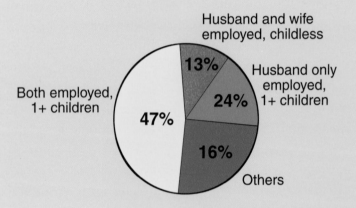

Husband and wife employed, childless

Both employed, 1+ children — 47%

13%

Husband only employed, 1+ children — 24%

16%

Others

JUNE 1976

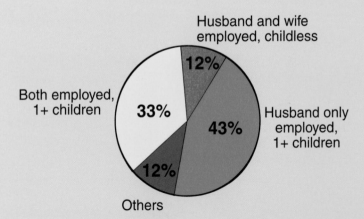

Husband and wife employed, childless

Both employed, 1+ children — 33%

12%

Husband only employed, 1+ children — 43%

12%

Others

Source: *Bureau of the Census*

Women were also making great progress in politics. The National Women's Political Caucus was formed to lobby for female representation in all government agencies as well as to support legislation of special interest to women. Shirley Chisholm (first African-American woman in Congress and a presidential candidate in 1972) said, "I have met far more discrimination as a woman than being black in the field of politics. . . . But, in spite of it all, I went to the Democratic convention . . . and began to open the way for women."[6] The National Black Feminist Organization, which insisted that "there can't be liberation for half the race," was formed in 1973. The following year, the Mexican American Women's National Association was created.

With women's presence and pressure, Congress enacted legislation favorable to the women's movement. Title IX of the 1972 Educational Amendments Act prohibited any college or university that received federal aid from discriminating against women. It also included a provision requiring female teachers and administrators to receive pay equal to that of their male colleagues'. Girls' athletic programs benefited greatly from these new laws, with new teams, locker rooms, and coaches making their welcomed appearance. The Equity Act in 1974 provided federal funding to assist schools in eliminating sex bias. Ivy League schools like Harvard, Yale, and Princeton started to admit women. In the face of several lawsuits, Congress passed a 1975 law requiring all service academies to admit women, and women began to enter the U.S. Naval Academy, the U.S. Military Academy at West

Point, the Air Force Academy, and the U.S. Coast Guard Academy.[7]

Changes in the Family

The increasing numbers of women with young children entering the workplace prompted reconsideration of roles within the family. "I was fifteen in 1976 when my mother got a job as a speech therapist," Rebecca recalled. "My father had really mixed feelings about it. He kept saying how proud he was of her, but when she bought a new blender and paid for it herself, he was really upset. They argued about things like that a lot, but my mother didn't give in."[8]

Carole's mother, like many other African-American women, was already working in the 1970s, but, said Carole,

> I was always the one asked to get dinner ready or dry the dishes, never my brother Ray. Then, when I was about 14 [in 1973], my mom become a real women's libber [a supporter of the women's movement also known as the movement for women's liberation]. She started talking about raising a feminist son and an end to role stereotyping [giving boys traditional male tasks and girls traditional female tasks]. So now Ray had to share in the housework. Plenty of times he tried to squirm out of it. Once he even tried to bribe me to clean his room, but I didn't. I felt like I had my rights.[9]

Carole's rights found support in a large segment of the popular culture dedicated to advancing women's issues. Feminist *Ms.* magazine, which began in 1971 as a section in *New York* magazine, had a circulation of two hundred thousand and a long list of advertisers by 1973. Slowly, the television

*A*uthor and activist Gloria Steinem attended a reception on March 22, 1999, to celebrate the rebirth of *Ms.* magazine. The magazine will now be owned and managed by women after years of corporate control.

shows of the 1950s, exalting the traditional male-dominated household—*I Love Lucy, Leave It to Beaver, Father Knows Best*—were replaced with shows written specifically for female stars, such as *Maude, Mary Tyler Moore*, and *Rhoda*. Movies such as *Alice Doesn't Live Here Anymore* gave credit to the determination and strength of single moms, and Diane Kurys' *Peppermint Soda* was a tribute to girls reaching adolescence.

An Unfinished Agenda

For all the ambitious attempts of feminists to span the divide of class, race, and sexual orientation, the women's movement of the 1970s was largely white, middle class, well-educated, and heterosexual. There were groups such as the National Black Feminist Organization, but, in general, women of color often felt that any demand for their rights as women would be a betrayal of their men who were simultaneously fighting oppression of their people.

Challenges to the women's movement came from lesbian and bisexual women who criticized its agenda as overwhelmingly beneficial to the heterosexual community, and from working women who complained about minimal attention to their demands for low-cost, quality child care and equal pay.

As women's groups moved through the 1980s and 1990s, they began to address the needs of women who were poor or from minority backgrounds. Still, change has not been even among all groups. Ethnicity, social class, marital status, and sexual orientation still remain primary determinants of what happens to women in American society. Sisterhood is powerful, but it is not yet universal.

Chapter 3

Still a Vital Force

$\mathbf{A}$t a recent meeting of a high school women's issues club, the group watched a video showing the dangers facing adolescent girls in different countries around the world. Several boys had attended the meeting, and after seeing the video, a lively discussion followed. As one ninth-grade boy was leaving the room, he commented to the club's advisor, "This wasn't at all what I expected. Everyone was so nice to the boys in the room. I thought you'd be kind of mean and angry, like feminists."[1] This stereotypical view of feminists as hostile, male-bashing women is one that is shared by many Americans, regardless of age and sex. A recent poll in *The New York Times* showed that most people believed that women's status had improved over the past twenty-five years, but the number who thought being called a feminist was a compliment was cut in half since 1992.[2]

Antifeminist Feelings

Several factors have contributed to the bad press the word feminist has received. One of the main reasons people became critical of feminism had to do with the economic recessions of 1973–1975 and 1982–1983. With the downturn of the economy, the manufacturing sector (male dominated) shrunk dramatically. Between 1978 and 1983, 3 million manufacturing jobs were lost. Women, for all the changes of the women's movement, still remained in the service area as waitresses, clerks, and salespeople.[3] Their entry into the labor force had nothing to do with the loss of male jobs, but many people blamed feminists for taking jobs away from men.

In this setting, antifeminism and the New Right (a vocal group of conservative, and often religious, Americans who want to see a return to traditional roles for men and women) arose, renewing the debate about the proper meaning of gender and women's place in society. One of the most influential critics of the movement for women's rights was Phyllis Schlafly. Schlafly, a political activist, started her own newsletter, *The Phyllis Schlafly Report*. She labeled feminists "a bunch of bitter women seeking a constitutional cure for their personal problems."[4] In her many talks across the nation, she echoed the sentiments of housewives and working-class women who felt belittled by the attention the women's movement had given to professional women.

The New Right, which found allies in the Republican administrations of both Ronald Reagan (1980–1988) and George Bush (1988–1992), furthered the backlash against feminists. Claiming to represent a "moral majority of Americans," the New Right charged the feminist agenda as being antifamily, antichildren, and proabortion.

*P*hyllis Schlafly speaks at a conference organized by conservative Christian groups to discuss social and spiritual issues.

The Defeat of the ERA

The New Right joined with antifeminist forces to oppose the Equal Rights Amendment (ERA), which was passed by Congress in 1972 and sent to the states for ratification. (Three fourths of the states have to ratify, or approve, an amendment to the Constitution in order for it to be accepted.) The ERA states that men and women have to be treated equally under the law. It was first introduced in Congress in 1923. To the various feminist groups that wanted the ERA passed, its meaning was largely symbolic, since the nation was already committing itself to supporting equality between the sexes. The opposition,

Women Working Together

In 1974 seven women at *The New York Times* filed a sex discrimination suit, *Elizabeth Boylan et al* v. *The New York Times*, to the Equal Opportunities Commission charging inequities in hiring, promotion, and pay. The suit expanded into a class action for 550 female employees and was settled in 1978 in their favor.

Source: Kate Mills, *From Pocahontas To Power Suits* (New York: Plume, 1995), pp. 266-267.

however, gathering around Schlafly's National Committee to Stop the ERA, warned of coed public bathrooms and the drafting of women into the armed forces if the amendment were passed. The committee's theme was "Defend the family and preserve the differences between the sexes." Their message found a receptive ear in the South, where eleven states voted against it and ultimately blocked its passage in 1982.[5]

Backlash

The intensity of opposition to feminism led the Pulitzer Prize-winning reporter Susan Faludi to state that there was an "undeclared war against feminism." In her best-selling book *Backlash* (1991), Faludi blamed the popular culture and the media for turning men and women against feminism during the 1980s.[6] More subtle but equally powerful was the publication in 1986 of the Harvard-Yale marriage study that claimed that a college-educated woman of thirty had only a 20 percent chance of finding a husband; by age thirty-five it was 5 percent. Some women wondered if they were not really better off in traditional roles.[7]

Divisions in the Women's Movement

Divisions within the women's movement itself added to the sense of confusion. As women entered the public arena, they encountered and reported increasing incidents of sexual harassment and date rape. Arguments for protection against this kind of abuse have gained criticism from clusters of feminists impatient with women's status as victim. Another group, calling themselves power feminists, argue for networking and using money to promote political change.

Problems Faced by Young Women

While this infighting has turned some women away from feminism, there are still many problems associated with being a young woman in American society. Since 1974, the rate of assaults against twenty- to twenty-four-year-old women has increased by 48 percent. More than 50 percent of women having legal abortions are between the ages of twenty and twenty-nine. And, there are growing restrictions on access to abortion. Many members of the New Right have vowed to overturn *Roe* v. *Wade*, or at least pass legislation to make it difficult for a woman to get an abortion. In 1992, in the case of *Webster* v. *Reproductive Health Services*, the Court, while not overturning *Roe* v. *Wade*, allowed state legislatures to place numerous restraints on women's right to choose an abortion.[8]

Of those women under the age of thirty-five who head households, more than half live in poverty. And while women earn the majority of college degrees, twenty-five- to twenty-nine-year-old women earn 76 percent of male salaries and the numbers go down with age.[9]

A Third Wave Emerging

In spite of the media attention to the differences among women, some young women and girls are finding many areas of common ground. Sarita Gupta, age twenty-one, attended a Feminist Expo dedicated to bridging the gap between generations of women. "Unfortunately there are a lot of myths and baggage around feminism for younger women, but to continue the progress that earlier feminists made we need them and they need us."[10]

In many areas, the difference between how males and females are treated in society is growing, and some feminist groups are trying to do something about it. NOW is consciously reaching out to girls and young women by holding meetings in different parts of the country that focus on a variety of topics, including rights of lesbians, girls and the media, body image, and making sure schools are gender equitable.

Young women who want to identify with feminism but do not like the label have started to call themselves Third Wavers, for the third wave of the women's movement. *Womanism* is a term preferred by some African-American women, and other women simply like the expression Women Moving for women who get things done. Melissa, an eleventh grader who attended NOW's Young Feminist Summit held in Boston in February 1998, said, "I personally like the word feminist. In fact, I'm proud of it. When you get down to it, it doesn't matter what we call ourselves as long as we keep fighting for the rights of women."[11]

Chapter 4

What Will the Millennium Bring?

One important priority for feminists in the 1990s was helping girls and young women resist the limiting social messages found in popular culture that told girls how to look and how to behave. Mary Pipher, psychologist and author of the best-selling book *Reviving Ophelia*, calls it a "girl poisoning culture" that sees femininity and self-reliance at odds.

Teen Culture

American teens receive a large amount of their culture from watching television—on the average more than five hours a day.[1] "[TV] has an important impact on teenagers, teaching them how to dress and talk and how to relate to work, school, adults, and family,"[2] explains Pipher.

Many television shows, however, help to reinforce negative images of women and girls. Jasmine Victoria, a New York City teenager, is critical of the way the media depicts her peers. Girls are hardly ever at the center of the story and are "portrayed as weak and helpless."[3] Others agree. In one poll, most women questioned thought that television stereotyped them as young, passive, dependent, and beautiful.[4]

In many popular television shows, the girls are competitive with one another over their appearances and their boyfriends, and are downright mean to one another. Shows that revolve around girls being supportive and nice to one another are few and far between.

Popular music and music videos, especially the lyrics to some rap songs, portray demeaning images of women. Stacy, a thirteen-year-old from Ohio, complained about a conversation she had with some of her friends. "We were talking about songs which actually glorified sexually abusing your girlfriend and the boys in the cafeteria thought it was funny. They just didn't understand why the girls were so upset by it."[5]

The sexualization of girls (seeing girls and young women only as sexual objects rather than as full people) has long been a complaint of the women's movement. But this sexualization is still very present in teen culture. Video games, usually marketed to boys, have recently introduced Lara Croft, a computer-generated action heroine in one of the most popular video games on the market. Lara is strong and clever. However, she is not being promoted as a role model for girls but as a sex symbol because of her ample measurements: 38:24:34.[6]

Eating Disorders

As a result of the popular culture that urges women, above all else to be thin and beautiful, the body may become the target of a young woman's emotional discontent and inner rage, says Maud Purcell a clinical social worker in Stamford, Connecticut.[7] This can take the form of eating disorders or a whole range of risk-taking behaviors.

The fashion industry has also created an unrealistic body image for young women. For several years, feminists have expressed concern that emaciated models' bodies are encouraging crash dieting, eating disorders such as bulimia (binging and purging) and anorexia (practically starving yourself), and low self-esteem.

When actress Alicia Silverstone appeared at the 1995 Academy Awards ceremony after having gained a few pounds, the press was very critical. The headlines, noting Silverstone's upcoming role in the movie *Batman and Robin*, blazed out "BATMAN and FATGIRL." For teenage girls, the message was clear. "What real women's bodies look like is labeled wrong and unattractive," said Los Angeles social psychologist Debbie Then.[8]

"Every morning I think about what I'm going to eat that day. I have an ongoing struggle with myself to eat as little as possible," said high school freshman Sarah Keenes.[9] "There's not a second in my life that I don't think about some aspect of how I look," confessed Sarah Goldberg, a high school senior.[10]

Loss of Self-esteem

Over the past several years, psychologists have written about the loss of self-esteem among young women. Self-esteem means the way a person feels about himself or herself. It comes from the way you feel about who you are and the value you have, and from the way others you think of as important feel about you. Several authors have suggested that girls

*A*fter being publicly insulted about a slight weight gain, Alicia Silverstone slimmed down for her role in *Batman and Robin.* She is shown here at the movie's premiere with, left to right, Arnold Schwarzenegger, director Joel Schumacher, Chris O'Donnell, and George Clooney.

lose feelings of self-worth as they grow from childhood to adolescence. Girls lose their optimism, confidence, resilience, and assertiveness. Instead, they become subservient, withdrawn, and unhappy.

The timing of the loss of self-esteem around middle school coincides with the physical changes that girls go through during their middle adolescence. As Dr. Andrea Marks, a specialist in adolescent health, said,

> [the] physical process and the psychological one are intertwined. Average girls at age 10 weigh 75 pounds; at 15 they weigh 125 pounds. Boys are also getting bigger, more muscular—but boys are

approaching the ideal of men in society, girls, by becoming bigger, are actually moving away from it.[11]

Dr. Emily Hancock, a psychologist in Berkeley, California, and author of *The Girl Within*, said that as girls move through adolescence, they "begin to think that they cannot measure up to the competition, especially the stereotypical waif-like image of the ideal American woman with a tiny waistline."[12]

Anxiety over body image accounts, some experts say, for the higher rate of depression among girls than boys. "Although depression rates before puberty are the same in boys and girls, at around age twelve girls start to have higher rates," said Dr. Myrna Weissman, a psychiatric epidemiologist at Columbia University. One survey reported that 27 percent of the girls questioned said that they were sad "many times" or "all the time." Others talked about crying a lot and having suicidal thoughts.[13]

Risky Behavior

Instead of trying to find help, many girls seek outlets for their sad feelings in risky behaviors such as

Self-esteem		
Both boys and girls lose self-esteem as they get older, but girls show a greater loss.		
	boys with self-esteem	girls with self-esteem
Elementary School	67%	60%
Middle School	56%	37%
High School	46%	29%

Source: American Association of University Women & Greenberg Lake Analysis Group, 1991.

smoking cigarettes, drinking alcohol, taking drugs, and becoming sexually active. For some girls, this behavior may also be a way of being accepted by their peers and trying to look more sophisticated.

According to a study published by the *Ms. Foundation for Women*, adolescent girls make up the largest group of new smokers. Girls often report that they smoke to lose weight. By age fifteen, more girls than boys report that they smoke. Over 40 percent of high school girls identify themselves as regular smokers and do not intend to quit. Other studies have shown that drug use is on the rise among females, and girls may be using drugs as frequently as boys.[14]

More young women are also turning to sexual relationships as a way of finding acceptance. In Sharon Thompson's book *Going All the Way*, based on interviews with four hundred girls, she notes, "Whenever they needed love, they could get it by having sex.[15] Studies show that the age at which girls are having sex is dropping. Approximately 40 percent of ninth graders have had sex. By the time they are in twelfth grade, it is 60 percent. About one million teenage girls become pregnant every year.[16] Nationwide, one teenage girl in ten gets pregnant every year, and after she gives birth to that baby, her life generally starts a downward spiral.

According to Barbara Defoe Whitehead, who has made a comprehensive study of sexual behavior in adolescents, "A single teenage mother is less likely to complete high school or to be employed than her nonmother peers and her child is at greater risk than other children for health and developmental problems and also for physical and sexual abuse."[17] It is also likely that the mother and child will live in poverty for their whole life.

In addition to pregnancy, there are other problems that result from teenage sex, such as sexually transmitted diseases. Early sexual intercourse is linked to cervical cancer and genital warts.[18] Also, girls who are sexually active before the age of fifteen tend to have more partners and are less likely to use barrier contraception, which places them at risk for sexually transmitted diseases, including HIV. The rate of reported syphilis cases among girls between the ages of fifteen and nineteen rose 112 percent from 1984 to 1991. As of 1991, the number of cases of HIV infection in adolescent girls has more than doubled, moving from 14 percent in 1987 to 39 percent in 1992. About one quarter of the forty thousand new HIV infections each year occur among thirteen- to twenty-one-year-olds.[19]

Teenage girls tend to have their first sexual experiences with male partners who are three or more years older, whereas teenage boys are likely to have their first sexual encounter with girls who are less than a year older.[20] This desire to be accepted may lead young women into abusive relationships. "As many as 30 to 40 percent of teenage girls in this country have been hit in the course of dating," says Dr. Eva Fiendler, the director of Psychological Services Center at CW Post Long Island.[21]

With so many pressures on girls and young women, it is natural to look to the school to help improve their confidence and sense of self-worth. However, many studies are finding that rather than helping to build a young woman's sense of self, schools are adding to the problem.

Chapter 5

Unequal Education

Children have many influences on how they grow and develop. School is an important influence because young people spend a great amount of their time there. That is why it is crucial for both boys and girls to receive an education that encourages them to fulfill their highest goals. However, many studies reveal that sexism pervades American classrooms and that it has a devastating impact on girls.[1]

Although girls enter school ahead of boys in almost every subject, girls graduate from high school behind in almost every subject. This lag is evident also in standardized tests, which are often important for college admission.[2] The difference in expectation and performance between boys and girls, called by many the gender gap, continues through college and graduate school.

How Girls Are Losing Out

As long as the gender gap exists in education, society is being denied the full talents of more than one half the population. Consider computer science. The National Science Foundation predicts that by the year 2010, 25 percent of all jobs will be technologically based.[3] Nevertheless, there has been a significant drop in the numbers of young women receiving both bachelor's and master's degrees in computer science. In addition, fewer girls are taking the Advanced Placement Computer Science Test in high school.

There is a social perception that scientific and technological courses are not for women. When Mattel's talking Barbie doll complained that "math class is tough," many parents and educators protested. But Barbie underscored the problem facing young women in traditional "male fields." Girls who have difficulty with computers or math are not encouraged to "stick with it, the way boys are," complained Ilana, a high school senior from New York City. "It's not considered that important because it's assumed she won't really need it later in life."[4]

Teachers are often unaware of the different messages they give to their male and female students. In one geometry class, the eight girls all sat in two rows, while the nine boys spread out over the rest of the room. Before class began, the teacher sat on one of the boy's desks and talked to the boys about the past weekend's football game. The teacher continued to make references to sports and the military as he taught the class. During the forty-five minutes of instruction, boys spoke thirty-two times and girls a total of twelve. In general, the girls raised their hands to be recognized, while the boys both raised their hands and called out the answers to questions. Not only did the boys dominate the discussion, but they received more positive feedback and encourage-ment. When a girl did not know the answer, the teacher merely went on to someone else. When a boy was uncertain, the teacher stayed with him and provided hints until he responded correctly. "I think that you really know this, Mark," he said on one occasion. "Try to picture it like a baseball diamond."[5]

This pattern appears to be fairly widespread throughout schools: Boys receive the majority of the teachers' attention and encouragement. To some extent, this bias is built into the curriculum and materi-als of most schools and the teaching styles of most teachers. Textbooks are usually written by and

*M*any people believe that Barbie dolls are poor role models for girls. Jeanette Williams, a teacher in New York City, does not allow Barbie dolls in her classroom.

about men. Women's experiences, perspectives, and accomplishments are generally missing from these books.

Many teachers emphasize competition and individual development in their classes, which can be alienating. Girls who have been traditionally raised to be ladylike and quiet are often reluctant to attract attention by waving their hands and calling out. They do best in classes that encourage cooperative or group learning, rather than those that reward competition and individual achievement. Cynthia Manhood of South Dakota recalled how assertive she was in school until fifth grade. "I was told by my teachers that my behavior before had been inappropriate, not like a young lady. It's amazing how influenced I was," she said, describing how she became too shy to speak in class for the rest of her secondary school years.[6]

"Going underground," "drowning," disappearing," "losing their voice" are the different ways in which experts have described what happens to girls as they go through school. This phenomenon also affects their participation in extracurricular activities. Typically, boys are much more likely than girls to participate in student government, be elected school president, and hold positions of leadership in school clubs.

While girls' athletic programs have benefited from enforcement of Title IX, inequities still exist. Girls reported that compared with the boys they had limited locker space, poor equipment, no continuity in coaches from year to year, and skimpy coverage in their school newspapers.[7] They have also reported sexual harassment in school sports.

Sexual Harassment

Sexual harassment is illegal both on and off the playing fields, but some studies have suggested that it is quite common within schools. In a 1993 study of sixteen hundred students in grades eight through eleven, 85 percent of girls said that they were sexually harassed.[8]

What exactly is sexual harassment? Sexual harassment is unwanted and unwelcome sexual behavior that interferes with a person's right to get an education or to participate in school activities. It may result from words or conduct that offend, stigmatize, or demean a student on the basis of sex.[9]

Many students know that if they fondle or grab someone's body against that person's wishes, it is wrong and violates the law. But sexual harassment can extend to other kinds of behavior as well. Teasing, name calling, writing graffiti on the walls of the bathroom, comments about another person's body, sexual remarks or suggestions, conversations that are too personal, pornographic pictures or stories, dirty jokes, obscene gestures, offensive displays of sex- related objects, staring in a way that seems too personal—all these can be considered sexual harassment.

While boys are sexually harassed, too, the

Sexual Harassment

Here are some things you can do to help stop sexual harassment:

✓ Think about how you feel

✓ Avoid being alone with that person

✓ Keep a record of what is happening

✓ Tell the person that you do not like it

✓ Talk to a friend

✓ Talk to someone in your family

✓ Talk to a school counselor

✓ Write a letter to the person, demanding the harassment stop psychological effects on boys are different. Seventy percent of girls, compared with only 12 percent of boys, said that the experience of being sexually harassed made them very upset. There are differences also in the educational impact for both boys and girls. More girls than boys report having difficulty concentrating in class and wanting to stay away from school.[10]

Michelle's experience, as she described it in her journal, is typical of many girls'.

> Before math class Ken and James were whistling at me in [the] hall. At first I thought it was kind of neat, then they wouldn't stop. I tried to ignore them and go to class, but they pinned me against the door and wouldn't let me go. I told them to get out of my way, but they just kept laughing and leaning against me. I felt real strange, kind of scared and mad at the same time.[11]

Although Michelle thought that this was no big deal, when Ken's winking at her and passing her "gross" notes in math class caused her to get into trouble with her teacher, she started to take his teasing more seriously. Michelle told Ken to stop but he wouldn't listen to her. Then things got worse. A series of prank phone calls were made to Michelle's home, then rumors about a "hot date" that she allegedly had with Ken began circulating in her school. Michelle became so upset that she started limiting her activities. "I don't even want to go to school,"[12] she wrote.

Michelle spoke to her friend Delores about Ken. Delores suggested that they go to their social studies teacher, Ms. Greene, who liked to talk to students. Ms. Greene took Michelle's problem seriously and brought Michelle and Delores to the school's complaint manager, Mr. Jefferson. (Many schools designate one or two people to hear sexual harassment complaints.) Together they wrote a letter to Ken, detailing everything that he had done and telling him clearly to stop bothering Michelle. Mr. Jefferson was there when Ken read the letter. At first Ken did not think that what he had done was so terrible, but Jefferson explained that if it had happened to him, he might feel differently.

After that, Ken and his friends left Michelle alone. It may have taken them time to understand that what they were doing was wrong, but Michelle was happy that she followed through on Dolores' suggestion. As Michelle wrote in her diary: "It made me feel good to know that I can stand up for my rights. I think some of the other kids feel I did the right thing."[13]

Chapter 6

Initiatives for Girls

Like Michelle, other girls around the country want to express what is on their minds. Some are doing it by creating their own homepages on the Internet or through their own publications such as *Blue Jeans*, which targets unrealistic body image, and *Get Real Comics*, which pictures girls playing soccer and boys baby-sitting.[1] *The New Girls Times* is dedicated to issues in which girls are interested, such as friendship, eating disorders, and the influence of the media on their lives. Similarly, *New Moon: The Magazine for Girls and Their Dreams* is another publication that helps break through sexist social messages, such as misguided ideas that girls are not good in math and computer science or that girls must all conform to a uniform body size and shape.

Mothers and teachers are helping girls to have their voices heard. Several schools around the country have initiated Women's Issues Clubs, Mother-Daughter Dinners, and Women and Girl nights at their schools. At The Wheeler School in Providence, Rhode Island, teacher Catherine Reed and some of her female students instituted Women and Girls Night in response to complaints by the girls in her English class that they were being silenced by boys in the classroom. At this event, they discuss topics such as date rape and female role models.

Girls and Women Together

While it is critically important for girls and young women to find their voices, it is equally important for them to be able to speak with someone they trust. Girls, Inc., an organization that has branches in 133 different parts of the country, helps put girls together with adult women. Isabel Stewart, director of Girls, Inc., said they help girls avoid engaging in risk-taking behaviors. According to Stewart, "If a girl can have someone she trusts telling her the truth about the options and pitfalls she faces, she feels more confident to face the world."[2]

The interest in supporting girls' strengths and talents, in taking them seriously and bringing them into the adult world was part of the thinking behind *Ms.'* Take Our Daughters to Work Day. When girls are welcomed into the workplace, and encouraged to ask questions, they "see that women have a range of life options."[3]

A New Women's Movement

This is a complicated time to be a girl. There are more opportunities than ever before. Girls can attend a wide variety of educational institutions and pursue a range of career and professional paths. They can look forward to expanded roles in their families, work, and government. Girls and women are learning how to have greater control over their bodies and their health care. There are many laws

*N*ine-year-old Angela Adams, right, gets a lesson in heavy machinery from her mother on Take Our Daughters to Work Day.

that protect girls and women from discriminatory practices at school and in the workplace.

But there are also many obstacles in the way of full equality with men. In general, men still have economic, social, and political advantages over women. And women of color and poorer women do not enjoy the same advantages as white middle-class women do. Some discriminatory practices— such as a teacher calling on boys more often than girls—are not illegal, often not obvious, and are difficult to change. Cultural and social attitudes that continue to see women in stereotypical ways endure. The media's persistence in perpetuating an "ideal," unrealistic image of young women has created a harmful cultural climate for many girls. The low enrollment of girls in computer science classes and their confidence in technology fields may limit their job opportunities in the years to come.

Obstacles, however, can also be challenges and calls for change. Sometimes isolated acts by

National Women's History Month

In 1987, Congress passed a joint resolution declaring March to be National Women's History Month. During this yearly celebration of women's past and present accomplishments, various community groups such as the Girl Scouts, women's advocacy organizations, and schools plan special workshops and programs of interest to girls and women. Some states have established a "Women's Hall of Fame," and others feature local women who have gained prominence in their communities. How does your school celebrate Women's History Month? For more ideas, contact:

National Women's History Project,
7738 Bell Road, Windsor, CA 95492

individuals or small groups are what is needed to create change; at other times, mass efforts are required. The history of the first two waves of the women's movement is rich in examples of different ways to improve the status of girls and women. Will the Third Wave of the women's movement continue to grow in strength? What form will it take? Will it be successful in changing some stubborn sexist attitudes about women? These are questions that the girls and boys of the present, will have to answer.

Introduction

1. Kristen Golden, "What Do Girls See?" *Ms.*, May/June, 1994, p. 56.

2. Daniel Goleman, "Why Girls Are Prone to Depression," *The New York Times*, May 10, 1990, p. B15.

3. *Body Politic: Transforming Adolescent Girls' Health*, Report of the 1994 Proceedings of the Healthy Girls/Healthy Women Research Roundtable, *Ms.* Foundation for Women, pp. 7–9.

4. Anna Quindlen, "Preparing for Womanhood Begins in Girlhood," *The New York Times*, April 8, 1993, p. A20.

5. *Body Politic*, p. 9.

6. Myra Sadker and David Sadker, "Sexism in the Classroom, From Grade School to Graduate School," *Phi Delta Kappan*, March 1986, p. 514.

7. Conference at Marymount College, Tarrytown, "Women, Girls, and Technology," November 7, 1970.

8. Carey Goldberg, "M.I.T. Acknowledges Bias Against Female Professors," *The New York Times*, March 23, 1999, p. 1.

9. Ibid.

10. Ibid.

Chapter 1. Background of Today's Women's Movement

1. Sue Heinemann, *Timelines of American Women's History* (New York: Berkley, 1996), p. 169.

2. Carol Hymowitz and Michaele Weissman, *A History of Women in America* (New York: Bantam Books, 1978), p. 98.

3. Heinemann, pp. 20–21.

4. Hymowitz and Weissman, p. 226

5. Ibid., p. 277.

6. Ibid., p. 284

7. Author interview. Last name changed.

8. Hymowitz, p. 312.

9. Ibid.

10. Sara M. Evans, *Born for Liberty* (New York: The Free Press, 1989), p. 222.

11. Elaine Tyler May, *Pushing the Limits* (New York: Oxford University Press, 1994), p. 30.

12. Hymowitz and Weissman, p. 313.

13. Ibid., p. 326.

14. Ibid., p. 328.

15. Penny Colman, *Fannie Lou Hamer and The Fight for the Vote* (Brookfield, Conn.: Millbrook Press, 1993), p. 15.

Chapter 2. Milestones of the Women's Movement

1. Amy Swerdlow, "Ladies' Day at the Capitol: Women Strike for Peace Versus HUAC," in Vicki L. Ruiz and Ellen Du Bois, eds., *Unequal Sisters* (New York: Routledge, 1994), p. 479.

2. Author interview. Name withheld.

3. Sara Rimer, "They Talked and Talked, and Then Wrote a Classic," *The New York Times*, June 22, 1997, p. 27.

4. Sue Heinemann, *Timelines of American Women's History* (New York: Berkley, 1996), p. 134.

5. William H. Chafe, *The Road to Equality: American Women Since 1962* (New York: Oxford University Press, 1998), pp. 89–90.

6. Heinemann, p. 83.

7. Ibid., p. 264.

8. Author interview. Last name withheld.

9. Author interview. Name withheld.

Chapter 3. Still a Vital Force

1. Author observation. Last name changed.

2. Sarah Boxer, "One Casualty of the Women's Movement: Feminism," *The New York Times*, December 14, 1997, Week-end, p. 3.

3. Sara M. Evans, *Born for Liberty* (New York: The Free Press, 1989), p. 303.

4. Ibid., p. 272.

5. William H. Chafe, *The Road to Equality: American Women Since 1962* (New York: Oxford University Press, 1998), pp. 100–104.

6. Nancy Gibbs, The War Against Feminism," *Time*, March 9, 1992, p. 50.

7. Ibid., p. 52.

8. Chafe, p. 134.

9. Karen Avenoso, "Feminism's Newest Foot Soldiers," *Elle*, March 1993, p. 116.

10. Karen De Witt, "New Cause Helps Feminists Appeal to Younger Women," *The New York Times*, February 5, 1996, p. A10.

11. Author interview. Last name withheld.

Chapter 4. What Will the Millennium Bring?

1. Jane L. Levere, "Advertising," *The New York Times*, June 11, 1996, p. D8.

2. Mary Pipher, "Bland, Beautiful," *TV Guide*, February 1, 1997, p. 22.

3. Kristen Golden, "What Do Girls See?" *Ms.*, May/June 1994, p. 58.

4. *Psychology Today*, quoted in Pipher, *TV Guide*, p. 22.

5. Author interview. Name withheld.

6. N'Gai Croal and Jane Hughes, "Lara Croft, the Bit Girl," *Newsweek*, November 10, 1997, p. 82.

7. Gabrielle Birkner, "Girls Are Number One," *The New Girls Times*, vol. 1, no. 5, p. 5.

8. Karen S. Schneider, "Mission Impossible," *People Magazine*, June 3, 1996, p. 66.

9. Ibid., p. 67.

10. Ibid.

11. Talk given by Dr. Andrea Marks, April 10, 1998, Women's Issues Club Dinner, Horace Mann School, Riverdale, New York.

12. Jane E. Brody, "Girls and Puberty: The Crisis Years," *The New York Times*, November 4, 1997, p. F9.

13. Daniel Goleman, "Why Girls Are Prone to Depression," *The New York Times*, May 10, 1990, p. B15.

14. Sabrina F. Hall, "Lighting My Fire," *Newsweek*, October 10, 1994, p. 11.

15. Sharon Thompson, *Going All the Way* (New York: Wang & Hill, 1995), p. 24.

16. Susan Black, "Sex and the Public Schools," *Executive Educator*, June 1995, p. 38.

17. Barbara Defoe Whitehead, "The Failure of Sex Education," *Atlantic Monthly*, October 1994, p. 69.

18. *Body Politic: Transforming Adolescent Girls' Health.* Report of the 1994 Proceedings of the Healthy Girls/Healthy Women Research Roundtable, *Ms.* Foundation for Women, p. 8.

19. Ibid.

20. Whitehead, p. 76.

21. Lawrence Kutner, " Parent & Child," *The New York Times*, November 14, 1991, p. 2.

Chapter 5. Unequal Education

1. Myra Sadker and David M. Sadker, *Failing at Fairness: How American Schools Cheat Girls* (New York: Scribners, 1994), p. 13.

2. Ibid.

3. Quoted in a letter from Ellen Silber and Jeane Bodin of The Marymount Institute for the Education of Woman & Girls, invitation to a conference on Women, Girls & Technology.

4. Author's observation of class.

5. Charles S. Clark, "Gender and Education," *CQ Researcher*, June 3, 1994, vol. 4, no. 21, p. 483.

6. Kate Stone Lombadi, "Women in Sports Still an Issue," *The New York Times*, November 17, 1996, p. 1.

7. Ibid.

8. Nan Stein, "Stop Sexual Harassment in Schools," *USA Today*, May 8, 1995, p. 1.

9. "Hostile Hallways," p. 17.

10. *Tune In To Your Rights* (1985), p. 2.

11. Ibid.

12. Ibid., p.17.

13. Ibid.

Chapter 6. Initiatives for Girls

1. Jennifer Weiner, "Girls' Magazines: All the Edge That's Fit to Print," *Star Ledger*, April 27, 1997.

2. Kristen Golden, "What Do Girls See?" *Ms.*, May/June 1994, p. 61.

3. *Take Our Daughters to Work*, *Ms.* Foundation for Women (flyer).

Books

Archer, Jules. *Breaking Barriers: The Feminist Revolution From Susan B. Anthony to Margaret Sanger to Betty Friedan*. New York: Puffin Books, 1996.

Dee, Catherine. *Who Says Girls Can't?: The Girl's Guide to Women's Issues*. New York: Little, Brown, and Company, 1997.

Heinemann, Sue. *Timelines of American Women's History*. New York: Berkley Publishing, 1996.

Mass, Wendy. *Women's Rights*. San Diego: Lucent Books, 1997.

O'Donohue, William. *Sexual Harassment*. Needham Heights: Allyn and Bacon, 1997.

Orenstein, Peggy. *School Girls: Young Women, Self-esteem and the Confidence Gap*. New York: Doubleday & Company, 1994.

Sadker, Myra, and David M. Sadker. *Failing at Fairness: How America's Schools Cheat Girls*. New York: Macmillan Publishing Co., 1994.

Wekesser, Carol, ed. *Feminism: Opposing Viewpoints*. San Diego: Greenhaven Press, 1995.

Internet Addresses

The Feminist Majority Foundation Online. 1999. <http://www.feminist.org> (August 16, 1999).

Girls Incorporated. 1998. <http://www.girlsinc.org> (August 16, 1999).

National Organization for Women. n.d. <http://www.now.org> (August 16, 1999).

The National Women's Hall of Fame. August 8, 1999. <http://www.greatwomen.org/index.html> (August 16, 1999).

New Moon Publishing. 1999. <http://www.newmoon.org> (August 16, 1999).